Also by Wayne Koestenbaum

# Stubble Archipelago

Published by Semiotext(e)
PO BOX 629, South Pasadena, CA 91031
www.semiotexte.com

Cover: Wayne Koestenbaum, *Blue Self-Portrait*, 2022.

Design: Hedi El Kholti
ISBN: 978-1-63590-206-8

10  9  8  7  6  5  4  3  2  1

Distributed by the MIT Press, Cambridge, MA, and London, England.
Printed and bound in the United States of America.

# Stubble Archipelago

Wayne Koestenbaum

Semiotext(e)

# Contents

*sempre* Steve

.

# #1 [How men eat]

How men eat ground beef
        porridge. How
men subtract themselves
        from ground beef porridge
        already in process.
Question the relevance of erotic
        triangles to the porridge
        men stir. Question
porridge, men, promiscuous—
        fill the question bucket.

Libraries transitioning to women
        lose their latrines,
paradise urinals betraying my
        gnomic squint,
capitalism's thrum tsk-tsking
        me because a twisted
        guillotine.
Herr Turtleneck, heir or hair
        poet-hope's couture
        circumvents calamity—

unfolding now to you who broach
      the nasal bulletin-board.
STEM he prophet-said, beard STEM
      he Beethoven-mumbled.
To murmur, its soup, I hearkened,
      aloof biceps-harpooning strategy.

Chiasmus grapefruit, squeezed, leaks no emotion—
      post office mouth gutter-stuffed.
Sculpt the ease, perfidy like
      toe jam inferno-feared.
*Répétez* goes the umpteenth ballerina,
      the hot cross bun of her or him.

# #2 [Eye doctor wanted]

Eye doctor wanted (at last) my cock
        combined with four-
        hand Mozart sonatas—
his tall Norwegian wife, caftan, in
        bed with us for
        novelistic complexity.
Chocolate chips, raisins, cashews in dish
        daughtered up my three-
        o'clock disappearance.
Time to teach math, ninth graders—
        my outlaw bike-ride hill
        a milkshake homo-reverie,

forehead coign-angle legatoing
        me into world peace
        treaty dissolver or solver.
Magnet dream told in St. Louis undoes how
        hinge-folds kill you
        minus Samothrace appendage.
Weathercock gaming his ass, I
        said, "You're gorgeous,"
        to no inkling-avail,
like kindling tossing homo down
        Brothers-Grimm-hill's Lotte
        Lenya aunt-lip fissure.

Treacle, damage me, then reverse the scar,
        drop basted turkey
        on Kissinger foot—no
peace in "did they fuck?" speculation cramming
        his memento mori pubes
        backward to canker-Eden.
Grail comes back, scar no impediment,
        gummed shame-salami
        mispronounced, samizdat lice-poem.

Tinkle the fairy Ark-rope wizarding
        stained cruelty-daughter,
        now regal-aged Cassandra.
Cram him up, celebrate him crammed,
        revise the cramming,
        call the cram *cream*.
How redux can you make East Germany,
        duckie? I get plumbed
        by rose-thorn, a Jekyll teething-ring.

# #3 [59th anniversary today]

59th anniversary today of Anna Moffo's
    Met debut.
House lone on mid-river island: no
    grocery delivery possible,
two-story Cheryl-crush house driveway-
    separated from boy
    Schwinn incursion.
Voyeur boy Brownie snaps girl-girdle,
    sissy's retribution mingled
    with laud. Drink

thy laudanum—treacle tit a boy too has,
    boy tit a god's rope-wrapped
    Ark, no Kristallnacht nigh.
Drizzle-streusel babka no palliative, a Ken
    doll cock-plateau, folded valley
    girdle-zone. Smell
G.I. Joe Levi's, raw denim, ass your
    "Tit Willow," D'Oyly Magna Carta,
    *l'oeil* Olive Oyl kiss'd.
Yr compresses, eye-infection babe, lick
    lidded orb if grilled
    cheese fails yr starved heart.

Stop sexpot locutions, anvil *esclave*-pressing
    your dented forehead—
    to desire concussion!
Second lone isle house, Shalott-ville like lump
    cello lower lip excreting-
    scraping Lalo, Fournier's.
*Roi* Lalo means piano-Mom lip-lump reprise—
    joy's chipped nail polish Joan
    Blondelling my Waterpik cavity

like when she flosses? or dentist digs curved
    implement to extirpate plaque?
Hot simulations if you scat-arrive in Astoria—
    queen in tub awaits groom
nuptial-piss arc hypothesized like Braille allegretto
    deathbed-shiver fingertip hyperesthesia
    —to unbesmirch my omphalos rainbow.

# #4 [Flatiron realness minus]

Flatiron realness minus sexual panic
      in your underpants,
         dreaming Tithonus codger.
Spiked abalone alabaster dopamine incites
      suicide terror, gun
         noose amyl nitrite.
Saké her cockhead his bologna if
      folk songs co-create
         Western narco-reality.
Our drug my drug our stomach our mis-
      prision outsweats karate
         lessons for Pa bonding.

Thousand sex partners giggle to Sontag it,
      Mercutio her, stigma
         him—pox-Mary hal-
         itosis alleluia.
Pink phlegm-card severs DNA helix, im-
      petigo colonized, de-
         cathected for diaper service.
Sweat-a-holic Laura Mars basket-weaver in
      art-therapy Paganini
         spittle—reckon thy

pudding, pinkie in tapioca bosom; cancer-recovered
     stalagmite-o-rama,
       I ♥ NY Brick-impotence

(Paul Newman), nose in his pubes. Noémie,
     Henry James's failed artiste, fecundates
     identification's sausage—
       his VD my *Tod*-relic.
"Liebestod" crackers w/ strawberry jam, ricotta,
     charnel-rumors? Arthritis
       tenderloin, 3 a.m. snack.
Body unpopular, gut a Mona Lisa cam-glimpse,
     jack-off Chekhov cues
       *Victor/Victoria* Weltschmerz-lees.

Negative space witch-calculus, Ghirlandaio
     teaches whip-widow
       a lady collar cholera
when Monet tinkles. FYI he intuits petrol-
     optics, boner-schism when
       chroma-spectrum unslackens
Jethro Tull—we played LP to lure
     smashed-lip sibling-alter-
       ego to drool upward, where
       Lord might await stretchmark-*Nacht*.

## #5 [Frizz-hair poodle lapdance]


Frizz-hair poodle lapdance obsequy,
    urinary libation-
        bearer gavotte I desire.
Lime-green Isadora-scarf, *Constipated Women*—
    Warhol's earliest ghost hugged
        me, unsmiling muscle-
cologne, clone-Köln trans chignon, his
    wart, what r u
        into? breed me?
No, sorry, I don't breed. Old meistersingers
    pound. Rivet the Ur-strip,
        urine iconostasis.

Pre-cum, he says, Mister Kurtz, whose dog
    lapped me Stanwyck-
        ward, redux Thaïs Bauhaus-boy.
"Méditation" golden shower Torah-Campari
    Stanwyck lockjaw—
        lips move, not teeth—*Big*
*Valley* pants-suit Circe. Begged twice for
    one "Signore, ascolta!" afternoon-pie,
        Licia nervous, tongue-Liù.
Sticky juice, my habitat pudding, sti-
    chomythia tinkling also—
        Lady Anne + hunchback,

discontent winter'd him *tramezzini*, like sandwich-
    ableism, Jo Van Fleet
    Abel-Mom kissing Cain.
Stutter worsened, odorous Lincoln Logs the for-
    feited Ding Dong, chocolate
    Instant Breakfast Karenina.
Strychnine, party of two, corner banquette,
    bedsores-to-go,
    cable TV hoodlum-speak.


I get happy violin Perkins-School-for-the-Blind-esque
    Stritch-ish dot com
    VistaVision vaginally
completes Kreme. Cruller u never lusted after. Corridor
    of day holds what
    Jackie Kennedy suffering
overheard at retrospective? Baby touches
    Brillo, I lose ethical
    compass, onanism *con ragù*.

# #6 [The artist sang]

The artist sang Jewish/Muslim prayers
    as mourners walked
    medicated down Seventh.
Friedkin's *Cruising* odor of Polo cologne near Jefferson
    Market Library clocktower
    and shut femme-prison.
Stasis of waiting on the top floor where nobody
    solicits your stippled bottom.
Fabulous posses cultivate
    émigrés, limpidity, besideness.

Blue Xmas-tree lights, yr bulbousness oppresses.
Dressingroom trailer door, a mitzvah
    never changing, says "Desi."
Rice grains arraigned on a plate, goats
    distant on a hill.
Eggplant, canned tomatoes, parsley, portents.
    Largo footsteps
    to the hospice.
Lone glove poised aloof on sidewalk tree's
    bent steel protector.

Aliveness a consequence of other alive people
     attesting to your
     lifelikeness. Prematurely em-
balmed kvetch berates supermarket's automatic
     door for not
     automatically opening.
Neck-crepe sighted in café mirror: Delphic oracle
     mouth's V a prep-
     ositional precipice.

Two empty sleeping-pill bottles lie Gumby
     legs akimbo in Kleenex-
     stuffed silver bathroom-
     wastebasket urn.
Progenitor-breath climbing upward to castrato
     stratosphere undoes
     postcoital poppycock.
Whose bed? My anus happens in his hypothesis—
     Descartes-limned universe
     a curved spine's casket remedy.

# #7 [Books by Lana]

Books by Lana Turner's daughter, Cheryl
     Crane: *The Bad Always Die*
     *Twice, Imitation of Death,*
     *The Dead and the Beautiful.*
Message from colleague: "She has lost
     consciousness. It is not
     likely to return."
Finality scissors her away to crypts un-
     utterable—con-
       sequence smothers
       mind's electromagnetic
       G-spot id-gleam.
Brain closed off, pulse thickened, screw in
     back fills lungs in-
     opportunely, dry ice

blankness be mine. She dies, I become
     nausea-nerd, Joyce's
     Gerty, crosshatched,
     musically sforzando'd,
punctured by TB not AIDS
     not TB not cancer yes
     cancer yes all of the above.

Eagle, leather bar, Bar-Ilan, banned boys,
  wounded pear-stomach,
  bread stored in aged ague-cheek,
  pocketed elder food escutcheon.
Reading glasses laid on bedside table to
  withstand the flood
  archaic—Ark in
  sock drawer, giraffe transitional object.

Moffo sang "Io l'ho trapunta" (I quilted it?) in last
  recording before death,
  Montemezzi—maybe not
  the last? maybe dream-
  records, stored fantasy-trove
  in unresuscitable attic?
Dream of making fairy-glossed records
  before I die—"Widmung,"
  "Erlkönig," "Seule," "Amarilli"—
bathhouse promiscuity sonnet sequence
  fairy necklace linking
  nursery to untimely
  death *agilità* Dorothy
  tornado rainbow-spasm.

Wind-torn sex-club, only one patron, urine beer
  muscle trophies, disco
  requiem, guilt-sirop
  honey-cyclone, fisting-
  corner naught-world.

Blowing in bathroom—knock on door, angry
       bartender—interruptus
       i.e., e.g., forfeiting
       eruption, a verse
       death no Job bellows.
Kissed slut-lips tortured by Sade-dryness. Loving A's
       hardness, Z's flaccidity—
       Gethsemane alphabet, in-
       vestigative frenum-spelunking.

# #8 [O razor in]

O razor in the bathtub, glee
      reifies you—
      shampoo, too,
a species of Prometheus, promotes
      bubble déjà vu.
Loving my imaginary son, and fain in
      verse to tell.
"You lack vocal chops"—slur reverberates
      in Mies van der Rohe
      outhouse, a Big Mac
      chiming its grease bell.

Barbara Stanwyck is the Coit Tower on the hill
      of my discontent.
Slough of Despond is the coffee shop where I
      dine with Alan Ladd
gaslighting me into marriage, my hair
      a Stockard Channing
      (*Grease*) rooster-comb.
Dreamt she fixed a dead lamp just
      by touching it.

Hudson River blue contains umber
        and lead: slate
        Siegfried suicide-muck.
Conjugate Adorno: adorno, adorni, adorna,
        adorniamo… Steal
        moral turpitude from padre.
"Your pubes are a godsend," epistolary bait—
        "Star of David suspended
        in chest forest"—wanting
        praise to land in solar plexus.

Judge overrules objection to daily
        unpremeditated chromatic
        habits, drip-
        painting recidivism.
Crispbread's smooth soft underside, like arm's
        inner skin, privatized,
        unsexed: haptic
        regression's Daedalus maze.
Her death ratifies my smallness—negligibility
        of my unanswered
        earthly envelope.

# #9 [Regret's a clod]

Regret's a clod—pebble impurity—in soul-mesh:
      rinse scrim, render it
      deathbed-transparent.
Is *idyll* idle or iddle? Non-anti-Semitic lute-
      pluck'd lake we
      tremolo-pass.
Dance tune: "Love the gefilte fish you're with."
      Rock it, aunt
Brünnhilde, I wake thee from fire-circle—
      incest-lust-heft pumping
      heldentenor dura-
      tional duress.

Mensch of you in my turkey stuffing slays—
      perineum's suspension
      bridge, resolved.
Dreamt he returned, meaty prof
      at moribund school
      mailbox—dead letters,
      desiccated spouse, demented son.
Round mushroom-head of my heart you chop
      death you subdivide
      into half-moon minion-fillets.

We break ourselves apart to make new vision-
      biscuits out of
      nothingness. The circle wept

to hear itself described as rhomboid.
      Sever thought from action,
      unhinge circling
      reverie from deed.
I made gouache shapes on Thanksgiving be-
      cause I needed to re-
      member I was reputedly alive,
Hannah Arendt crooning Brahms
      lullaby over my Jason
      Gould pseudo-incest cradle.

Lemon zabaglione curve of me creates
      a nonsensical
      reason to dream backward.
Faux pas to ask for a blurber's copy: they dropped
      my praise from the book.
      No shame to be an
      omitted mouthpiece.
Why shouldn't seraphic stillness fill me, as if yr
      meat in the bathroom were
      messianic time's momentary
      emissary cracking me open?

# #10 [Upload to private]

Upload to private album the yellow baseball
      shirt photo wherein
      I look Botoxed.
Ladybug sentient yet stationary on Marimekko
      shower curtain's blue
      calyx flame.
Dreamt a gay literary critic reviled me, tore
      up my dorm room's
      paltry wall-to-wall carpet
      in Trilling rage-fit.
Hordes of like-minded Wayne-haters gathered in amphitheater
      to watch the slow
      unpiecing—sleep cure
      in gelid Alps a coddled gulag.

Nutty obscene tonic OCD Joan Crawford's
      *My Way of Life*'s
      stomach gurgles from
      unwise imaginary emetics.
Unallegorical withies, moving between white
      triangles, overlap
      an unevenly contoured
      square (it won't forgive you).

Osculum underwater wants my participation
        in immoral acts—tongue-
        drama, "Always up
        for getting blown, mister."
"How thick is it?" Thick enough to depopulate
        *Middlemarch*—white
        window-frame reflection
        on black-jacketed Merleau-Ponty.

Drapes acknowledge the slant "H" they bear,
        flashback swastika
        siphoned into
        Mondrian eyelid-specter—
eye's inside lid contains Mondrian
        swastika condensation. Paper
        bag pleats echo
        crucifix or nude Raphael
        Soyer limbs cut by horizon.
Lascaux butt, where human and antelope
        converge—glute muscle
        you'll scapegoat ("she
        let the ball drop"—
        career condemners).

What was the ball? Where did it drop?
        Crayon on coitus celluloid.
        *J'accuse* the male
        old fart, *moi, toi*—
        *trois contes* uncountable.

Neighboring rejector, actor, dancer, mustache,
  always a "th" in
  your name to the-
  atricalize its Irma Vep
  (Vilna?) Ludlam-plush.
Ghetto theater, curtain rod plunged into orifice
  named "me" for
  shorthand, explanatory
  ease—to lube the theorem.

# #11 [Green tuppence strewn]

Green tuppence strewn across a land
    that couldn't tolerate
    green tuppence.
Then my golden cookies came to the rescue
    of a damsel
    herself named Cookie.
Our boutique is rad. Call me bunion.
    Butt extends beyond
    where trousers end.
Dead woman rummaged through
    pocketbook at the top
    of the pocked stairs.

Ferocious stubble undoes wan
    pedestrian's equanimity.
Crying girl squelches urge
    to vomit beside aban-
    doned train trestles.
Black wire mesh around scaffolding depicts
    naked man's splayed
    crucified limbs—allegory
    aimed at gullet.

Maître d's pants—slayers—more snug
　　than plaid Presley
　　tart-pants I spent unpoetic
　　hours struggling to love.

Slain habitually by strangers'
　　atomizer-ambient
　　sexuality—my hobby
　　is mortification
by fleet comparisons. Poached egg's remnant
　　stickiness on upper
　　lip not an apotheosis.
Mr. Death, without brush or pencil you trace
　　rear's curvature.

*Elements of Style* discarded as rubbish in stairwell
　　pungent with chlorine
　　and kitty litter.
Unkind Robin around the block, girl I stigma-
　　named *carrot top*, my paisley-
　　femme revenge hemmed
　　in our shame kinship.
Do pilgrimage and predilection belong in the same
　　nervous system, and is
　　this photo offensive?

# #12 [Fruitlessly cruised flat-assed]

Fruitlessly cruised flat-assed beanie-and-wedding-
    ring-wearing man reading
    *Financial Times* on C train.
Bootless cries like coral-colored vinyl handbag dangled
    over inverted paradise's
    Cerberus dog-maw.
Death took me shopping for dildos and poppers—
    neophyte subordinate to
    Socratic anal-muse.
Mustard scarf over persimmon peacoat, woman in wind
    tunnel crosses loveless bridge.

Stalled in courthouse traffic near dead man's
    apartment—wilted
    lettuce in frigid sidewalk crates.
Reconceptualize sexual voracity as heuristic—
    meteorological soma-
    tests, anti-Thanatos.
Where highway puckers, imagine a cathedral—
    surprised, instead, by
    sanitation truck, windowless.
Bank ATM's ad-model looks like large-cocked
    dogwalker—shy smile
    creates indents below flash-eyes.

Red fire-extinguisher wheel-dial near discarded Marxism
    paperback and Lucite
    turntable without spindle.
Trans guy with hairy shoulders and chest scars, 5′3″,
    app pal, materializes on sandwich
    line: make a children's
    book of wiry curl-halo,
    jejune 'neath pressed-tin ceiling.
Woman w/ pink fake-fur coat, man w/ denim skirt—
    style snippets solace
    home-bent wanderer.

Orange-leaved tree's death-life interstice. Bananas
    five for a dollar: capital's bias.
    Folding underwear, a practice
    between dharma and sapphics.
Stranger-twink from 7,180 miles away,
    web-dweller, asks, "Please sir can you
    help me get out of my country
    and keep me with you?"
300 pounds says wow to headless photo
    but "I'm not looking,
    merely browsing"—
    defeated or redeemed, you decide.

# #13 [Bedside lamp reflection]

Bedside lamp reflection tripartite on cream wall,
        you contain *pli-*
           pleated innuendos, fathom-
           less caverns un-
           sounded by pillowcase.
Dog's tail resembles flapping human penis: I need
        to become better
           acquainted with all
           mammalian anatomy.
Chrysanthemum decal on trash chute neutralizes
        user's Anthropocene
        bad vibes. Garbage
        fecundity = ecocide.
"Because you're a sweet man I'll put one free
        orange in yr bag,
        boss." "No,"
        I say, "you're boss—
        we share boss status."

To be recused from the unfolding catastrophe
        even if I am
        its culpable author.
I stare at him on subway to offer love,
        not to colonize—

beanie, stubble archipelago
wrapped around ocean chin.
Bette Midler grayblonde locks of wife I betrayed—
my hair (eye-for-an-eye)
vanishing. Orange
peel encircles pavement's chewing gum.
Three pink plant-pots piled up. Woman on night stoop,
Henry Street, to sibyl-companion:
"I'm shaken to my core."


Met horn-object's dad—same kernel eyes, wry Zeus-
depth, squinting at son-
hair, soft son-chest I pressed,
stentorian ultimatum muted.
*Le vent est plusieurs*, for example, a several species,
avoids the tumult
of tangerine pointillist bra
laid sideways over Sand's grave.
Sent bulge to avowed bulge-lover: no response.
Paper bag marked by semi-
circles, psychotic rouge-dots,
Marcel Marceau born-in-truck
Gumm Giulietta *Cabiria* pathos.


Too many words shoved together, hyena-style.
Jane Freilicher's birthday
today. Frank's Jane. Jar
of petals, cockatoos, pomegranates.

Pizza-box stain's aster-star. Dried hydrangea's counter-
espionage. Arthritic toe.
26-year-old James Dean clone-face a Narcissus pond
without ripple, no smile
arrowed to my pubic-
cancelled gramps-visage.

# #14 [Mouth-shape blade-gouged into]

Mouth-shape blade-gouged into elevator's
    wood-paneled door.
Dreamt I was pallbearer for JFK,
    declined to kiss the widow.
Clutched couch-pillow to my torso, pseudo-
    pregnant at funeral—
    biomorphic plaything in
    my cerements bassinet.
My popo, curved and wind-sensitive as a Boeing
    747: nocturne's melisma
    requires flexible pivoting
    thumb on appoggiaturas.

Red colander's sprocket-holes an invitation
    to become a per-
    forated vessel, water
    jetting up my eyelet.
"Touch the first picture and it enlarges"—tip
    offered to any lust-object
    on World AIDS Day without
    art: ashamed of showing
    face but not cock.
If you never knew your father's parents,
    your father becomes
    more of a void.

Idol's perfume was White Shoulders:
    Walgreens flânerie
    revives her olfactory specter.


Spent sabbath titling neglected paintings:
    *Optimistic Prairie,*
    *Choir Island Constellation,*
    *Horizontal Fruit*
*Camp Landscape, Summer Figure Echoes on Orange*
    *Plateau, Antidotes*
    *and Caprices, Elementary*
    *Nocturnal Triangulation,*
*Rock Stars with Dream Companions, Idea Chair,*
    *Picnic Revelation, Alert*
    *Amulets.* Singing,
    emphasized "u" vowel.


Fauré *mélodies* album-spine is Duchamp
    Gioconda smile
    truncated, waterlogged.
Shadow of refusenik vase falls valse-like,
    hand puppet athwart
    egg table.
Five neck-wrinkles like Queen Elizabeth's
    collar, invective
    hurled by widowed
    duchess at my mourning
    leg's varicose rosette.

# #15 [Smiling lasciviously, carrying]

Smiling lasciviously, carrying oat lattes
      down war-torn street—
      sorry, wrong pedophile.
Restless waters versus restless waiters spritzing
      on the Zattere, envying
      atemporal gulls and Kim
      Novak's Santa Maria
      della Salute déjà vu
or Il Redentore, chunky apocalypse—identifying
      with power pressing
      trumpet-hand against
      my caries jaw.
Madison crosswalk: rich woman's pained, clenched face:
      how do I know she's rich?
      how know pained?

Massive flower-delivery outside St. Regis hotel—
      importunate uneventfulness.
Orange workboots, not waterproof, ricochet
      beggar's *auito*.
      *La vita perduta*—
      whose lost life? Half-mine.
Corner café: fantasized shoplifting
      smoked cinnamon milk
      chocolate bar and getting caught.

What sunset looks like when landscape pulls
        the metamorphosis
        trick on your eye.

Lispector says don't wait for the ideal
        moment to write;
        it never arrives.
Refuse exaltation, dream-bust
        offering two teased
        nipples, no rebuke.
I woofed the zeitgeist. Dialectical
        roulette. *Temps perdu*
        didn't woof me back.

Dreamt a skinny green spider crawled up my clothed
        body as I drowsily
        prepared to lecture
        on Donatello's *David.*
Swish sound of broken wooden match falling on tissue
        in trash can: unloved
        unmourned nonentity
        match, skinny nudnik.
Student asked, "What is a pogrom?" I paused,
        dispensed the medicine:
        "A mass slaughter,
        often of Jews."

## #16 [Edmund White mentions]

Edmund White mentions Georges Thill, whom I
    mentioned earlier today
    in another, lost
    context, never to be
    salvaged or forgiven.
Synchronicity dictates I must soon read Jean
    Giono's *Melville*.
    "Do you reach a guy's
    second hole?" bulge-lover
    asked, not precisely
    intending me as addressee.
"Do you have a mezuzah?" he asked,
    remembering tight
    turquoise underpants
    and their contents.
Rebuffed by former beseecher: turned off by
    neck, nose, age,
    alacrity? Faux-
    pursuit, a Maya
    game, sans saturnalia.

I invent a forgiveness button
            on my right index
            fingertip: whatever I touch
with my balm button receives
            temporary benediction
            lasting until the next
            instant I ask
the chorus for mercy. Ideal receipt-site for cure
            is my forehead. No one
            can turn to rubbish
            my digit's ability
to grant revocable clemency: anyone's
            dermis transmits a ripe
            peach's mystic authority.


Compared to Ariana Grande, The Archies
            sound like Schoenberg
            tied up and force-
            fed an overdose of Stevia.
Misheard "sticky buns" as "sissy buns." Yahweh,
            the walking em-
            bodiment of sapphism
            at its most terse.
Craft beer & fusion cocktails sold in Ludlow
            synagogue founded 1893.


Dreamt Virginia Woolf's Berkshires
            villa was mine: I issued
            letterpress invitations

to a sample sale held
in a fire-alarm-buoyed
subordinate mansion-in-training supervised by a mentally
ill warden. Cambridge
became zone of secret
finger-pressure applied in bathtub to Hanukkah
forehead: save me
a seat, Elijah, in your
muscular tub, O lavender
Medea a cad betrayed.

# #17 [Older I get]

Older I get, the more serious I become
     about wearing
     makeup and wig.
Caftan, too. Always interested in a rub, kind sir:
     love yr eyebrows.
     King Minos pix
     disguise age.
Blend turquoise, Sèvres blue, bluish purple: impose mix
     on passive quinacridone
     violet's impersonality.
Try to detect how clearly delineated
     "subject positions" find
     angles of mutual
     pleasurable accord without
     destroying each other.

Joan Rivers baking Xmas cookies seen sideways
     through tunnel window's
     mirror lake Simi-
     lac® simulacrum.
Every novel I love is fragile. Red stars
     on black duffel bag
triangulate with Lynn Redgrave's in-
     dependent sources of self-
     esteem, not harvested from *Lear.*
Wrongly seeking sublimity in barn-roof gutter crevice.

Lucent ceiling corrugations a dauphinois
            potato when his Pompeii
            gaze claims me, then disappears.
Carved kouros lips, stone lingerie, scandal
            pudding: congregated
            shames comprise a menu.
Hives on my calves await Purim-Benadryl's
            alleviation. Sob-collapse
            throws ash on coffin,
            lowered: crowded town
            car back from cemetery
            to capers, cream cheese.


Abstract expressionism is what happened at the hospital:
            fools disputing climate
            change, Tiffany-
            blue establishing-shot's
            concentrated inattention.
"I'm glad you gave up the figure," she said.
            Wrong. I haven't
            stopped pursuing nudes.
To be the dread golem, aloof in Prague, boning
            up on *feuilletonisme*,
            Eton peacoat toggles
            unclasping *gelt*-Jocasta.

# #18 ["Roar of God"]


"Roar of God," misread as "rear of God":
        imagine sepulchral
        buttocks, Ten
        Commandments cloven.
Met a guy named Luke Surprise: blue undies:
        no praise when I
        pulled mine down
        a half-inch, upholding
        deception's infernal reign.
Saw truncated (dismembered?) pumpkin on road. Teach
        seminar on essay
        films, genre gaily
        undefined. Second
half of pumpkin appeared further down winding
        road—mailbox groin
        where unscrutinized
        gay couple lives, Shirley
        Jackson hill haunting
        gloaming coral sky.


Dreamt Moffo sang Montemezzi live at Met, her voice
        teacher beaming
        in audience: I didn't go backstage
        afterward but hypothesized

Moffo's perfume. Bergamot?
Dreamt tried to buy peacoat for bedraggled Israeli
    gay on Mass Ave,
    our chosen specimen
    stolen from under us
    by rude conniving clerk.
Simmering cogitation today, chez moi, concerning
    Faye Dunaway's up-
    coming return to Broadway,
cancelled. Daven it. Anything
    can go in
    the language glove.


*Nostalgie de la boue* Washington Square "smokes,
    smokes, smokes"
    drug-trade retro-paradise?
Experimenting with social death as appetizer;
    social death as
    fish course, meat
    course; social death
    as incunabulum.
Looking up *architrave*, looking up *entablature*:
    indulging in rage
    capitalism for
    the heck of it.


Plath had no right to kill Plath?
    —world-soul nabbed
    in circumstantial theft.

Dildos as dowsing rods in Schwules Museum: handle
    with care on
    Sebald's Yahrzeit.
Quick cock-photo-bomb to Greek DJ as if King
    Tut commanded: Ros-
    icrucian Museum
    water lilies near
    synagogue not Monet:
    reincarnation, promised
    the mail-order sleaze-brochure.

# #19 [Blue tape seam]


Blue tape seam dividing debased sidewalk:
    piss there, despite
    sworn perv-abstinence?
Stop mentioning lifelong tropism toward swollen
    *Stollen* Swiss Miss
    misbegotten *Hello, Dolly!*
A literary version of hoarding disorder he asked me
    if I had: cardboard
    liquor boxes flattened,
    stacked, rope-tied.
Plastic-wrapped nuptial mattress dead on street: green
    gaffer's tape predicts
    spring's Dylan-Thomas-
    promised bog surge.


Her hennaed *Frühlingsnacht* hospice hair, a Bon
    Ami scouring job to undo
    Napoli hostel boy-
    teen flip-flop shuffle.
Passing St. Vincent de Paul, boarded up,
    incorrigible fire truck
    alarm ear-slashed
    my zither opportunism.
Hydrant water prick-plunges my sneaker mesh:

beggar mouth and tyrant
mouth gagged by dialectic.
Brutally Fitbit-interpellated, I fight bootless
back by fool-misplacing
wrist toy: reclaim it,
re-smooch w/ my
Fitbit jizz interpellatee.

Coveting your metallic sneakers, svelte flood-
trousered Puck outpacing
my origins-of-
totalitarianism lech amble.
Stanley Tucci lookalike, veer away, IV
not finding its vein.
In pj's she street-squats on milk crate, doyenning
over the auto-frigging
*moi*-daveners.

*Noli me tangere* anti-Semitism's mule-gait
a tapioca bubble I'll gum.
Radio's Ella Fitzgerald "Santa Claus Is Comin' to Town"
quashes (or syntagm-
bumps) my kindred's
Botox stigmata, Yuletide
Juvéderm, AZT
joy-enwrapt $-pubis,
or Richard Tauber's daffodils frost-seared:
*geliebt ermordet* Stars
and Stripes grave-kilt montage.

# #20 [My inexplicable bruise]

My inexplicable bruise, left forearm's contusion—
    from unkindness committed
    or received? Guilt's
    railroad-crossing bidirectionality.
Sepia hydrangeas receive pink glow from paper
    tulip's reflected updraft:
    Fallopian tube's blue cup
    lip ends its edge regime.
On subway, deranged man shouts to his tiny son,
    "I'm going to make you
    cry now. I've got to do it,
    because you don't listen."
Caressed Bacchus hand, without closure,
    hoping for furtive
    streetcorner grope, Buber-
    Scholem empathy Zion rub.

How do you build an 18-story apartment building?
    How do you love
    an 18-story apartment
    building you've barebacked, gurgling
    underground sedge-water
    as passacaglia continuo?

Dreamt that a writer who'd experienced social death
        commiserated with me
on a snowy mountain slope. Spider or slug
        crawled into my winter flannel
        sheets. Met teacher on grammar
        school tarmac to discuss
        labia's adjudication of gender-
        schism fisticuffs, I the slop-pit.
To repent silently, and then to give a paper on a panel
        about repentance:
        replay or undoing
        of original sin against
        progenitor's multipurpose-
        room *Traviata*, size D cups
        hole-puncturing my goldfish baggie.


Dusk winter sky reflected in cracked mirror, trash
        bundle inferno ramble,
        puppy-huddle pet-shop
        window's newspaper
        confetti: two penises
        it appears F.N. Souza
        has in self-portrait.
Nestle up to night's shelf as unto mammal teat's ledge—
        pirate inseminator
        abandoning you, quick
        stubble-mate one
        mercury thermometer bubble-
        drop away.

"Thanks! Face?" Leer near-post-
       humously at hair's
       phlegm concentration,
       cough's gristle rope
       hacking widow-trauma.

Prison and school: both loom hard
       against riot-
       tending horizon.
Short French dad, *moi*-parallel, wears red
       sister-boots, mama-
       stitched, not cruelty-free.
Stand up, father-brother *Zimmer*-squatter,
       fold your remorse
       into three particle-waves.

# #21 [Foment the railroad]

Foment the railroad, unsupervised child, tri-
  breasted—Herculean slight
  to Elektra fissure where
  father falsetto pink-harmonizes.
Smells like graham crackers: to worship
  graham crackers,
  to be defined
  by crumb research.
Draw lines seen eyes closed: excavate rectangles,
  triangles, half-circles,
  crosshatched tubes,
  curled connecting wires
  leather-misfiring:
  S/M dopamine flood.
Manet nipple Lascaux-splayed: mansplaining
  *L'Origine du monde* to
  Berthe Morisot: Falconetti's
  dirt sweat Ark sob
  + my Bardot mullet.

Saw you, Matt Damon, in my Oedipal Bermuda isosceles
  *Flaming Creatures* ass-
  periscope arising to push
  kingfisher's sprung *Dämmerung.*

Remembering Valley Fair Shopping Center apple cider
        and "fuckin'," exploding (like
        igloo tetanus-asterisk)
        filtered cider's detestable
        virgin-birth transparency.
Nancy Drew kvelling, "I'm the most voluptuous
        Palmer Method heroine,"
        chalkboard's air-raid siren
        phonetic Valkyrie
        groin-V atemporality—
        yet Iwo Jima Gregory
        Pecking me into Eichmann
        trial self-soiling.
*Performance* Jagger waist, The Who spectral dildo
        opening {my} lingual
        receptivity to preconscious
        Dreyfus dreidel bull's-eye.


Vomit-milk aroma exudes a heist comfort. Smear face
        with dog crap for
        confrontation-therapy sorbet.
        No limit to papa
        extradition's I-Thou charm.
Almost sniffed Bruegel man arm light-fleeced in aisle.
        Tabatha child witch cry
        a burin tool, engraving
        {my} mystic mirthful writing pad.
As raspberry tints yogurt, so remorse
        tints equilibrium's whey.

Historic poem writ on shame day, Tahnee Welch
     seeing mother Raquel in
     dream ideation's Jocasta
     cotton-candy cardboard stick.
Is a cookie a vegetable, is a steak a fruit,
     is a daiquiri an opera,
     is a legume an encounter group?
Black oil lines arrest brink's indecisive obelisks.

## #22 [Adorno gave me]

Adorno gave me, as stocking stuffer, this question:
  is art's protest
  "mute and reified"?
The day after a disqualified holiday is as night-
  marish as snake-
  pit Yule itself.
His vagina and her penis are my
  auld lang syne: please
  table "my"
  for the duration.
Butt-crack, male phenomenon, rampant in airport—
  disgusting or attractive?
  Hung jury.

Guinea pig must choose between rescuing a Rembrandt
  or a cat from a burning
  building. Pig picks
  the Rembrandt. It turns
  out to be a forgery.
"Scranton," story by a woman who died long after last
  time we spoke: no
  rift intended, just
  accident, attrition,
  baseless froideur.

Add her to roll call of dead friends never given a final
        summarizing statement—
stalagmite rapports no epitaphs etch.

Avoidance is mead, curse metamorphosed into a frieze's
        gladioli: the line
        between living and dead
        an unforeknown, un-
        folding habitat.
Dreamt novelist rode on float through Aix-en-Provence:
        cure blindness, I told her,
        by urinating on
        unseeing eyes.
Choose two nonfiction writers to pee on. *Vogue* elected
        her to model "New
        Narrative" Kohut-Bion-
        splitting shrink
        elegy glut.

Lacan's butt-crack, from the mother's point of view—
        "enjoy your meat!"
        Lick lips when meeting
        psychoanalyst Chrysothemis,
        plastic surgery my barb
        riposte when she re-
        bukes dye job.
Asynchronous on New Year's threshold, listening
        to Richard Tauber
        German folksong schmaltz,

1926 and 1931.
Dreamt I couldn't play a B-major scale. Steve dreamt
he designed an apartment
for Trump, who tossed
him a bottle of seltzer.

`

# #23 [It sounds parasitic]

It sounds parasitic when I hum
        pastiches of Fauré,
        Schumann, Bizet.
Watched documentary footage, violent dismembering
        of chicken and cow:
        colonial mimicry.
Why, in trance, does white foam stream from possessed
        mouths? Cotton, cornstarch,
        saliva, fruit: simu-
        lated aethereal cum-
        cream-of-wheat *écume.*
My grandmother sent me to the Jewish deli to buy
        World War One cookies.

Dreamt neo-Nazis set fire to warehouses on my block:
        reviled revelers
        flooded the streets.
"My manuscripts, in the burning building," I remembered,
        remorseful but not
        Parthenon-distraught:
        accustomed to annihilation.
My shrink gave out free vials of vinegar

at Boston's Back
Bay sodomy-transit station.
I wore a black skirt with a counter-
intuitively masculine
resemblance to rev-
olutionary culottes.

Dreamt I shaved my face with careless,
quasi-violent
inexactitude
and watched *Night and Fog*, a new version,
containing footage
of rickety red
Berlin house facades
my father or Walter
Benjamin might once
have passed. Dreamt
I tried to parallel park in Hudson while
overseen by a kleptomaniacal
(scarf-snatching) piano teacher's
*Pictures at an Exhibition.*

Discovering again the Creamsicle
attained by mixing
pink and yellow.
Wanting (yet failing) to plunge into Brecht
and thereby be
transfigured into straight-
forwardness and size.

Last line I wrote, negation flame-licked you: rewind January
to squeeze New
Testament lingual
unguent onto boil.

## #24 [Beard smooth skin]

Beard smooth skin foams into snub—forty
       minutes squandered
       as horn-libation for
       curt kouros.
Turned him lickety-split into sub bottom by feigning
       pique at his tardiness.
Darwinian survival-reversibility of damaged mother
       in dream where I
       ascended to Donne
       literacy inch-wise
       on summer kitchen's
winter porch: she, armistice-tranquil, stood by wood-rail
       awaiting potato-peeler
       father selling insurance

to reach Jell-O islet-isthmus in silver wedding-cup
       aloft, a retro-
       active berakah.
Dreamt shrink-novelist's white-black jewelry nestled its donnée
       into offered breasts—
       indifferent yet hos-
       pitable, subject to
       fingerprint impress.
Dreamt I fell asleep in a clawfoot tub and you

said my snores were
audible in the hallway.
Later we attempted asylum hill, TB retreat, Alpine
Siddhartha soul-loss
triangulated w/ early cinema
V-seat, Bertoia chair
if Mekas had love-filmed it.

Lithuania calls my cell phone, hangs up: next day,
I watch *Reminiscences*
*of a Journey to Lithuania:*
next day, Mekas dies.
I claim clairvoyant synchronicity: craving to be
enfolded within mystic
diary chain, lines
filmed or scribed, each
forgiven by duration's
monad-dram, teaspoon
or millimeter parentheses clipping memory segments, i-
solating then joining
synapses, babushka
Bolex the never-betrayed.

Rethinking the Ten Commandments as I walk to work
in the rain, especially
"honor thy," the
"honor" ambiguous,
a vanishing-point piazza
exercise in farsightedness.

Disturbing juxtaposition in grocery magazine-rack: Anne Frank
 commemorative issue +
 *Dogs: Why We Need Them.*
 Ask Anne? Ask the No One?
Saw murdered Gregory Battcock's handlebar mustache,
 hallucinated below horizon-
 line's plaint: GB washing
 his ass in Riverside Park
 between efficiently sandwiched tricks.

# #25 [Seen, discarded in]

Seen, discarded in stairwell: CorningWare casserole
      cover—glass, forever
      severed from the squat
      vessel it was meant
      to surmount.
Toward you, glass lid, I feel no pointed grief—
      but I acknowledge
      your isolation, urn
      for pot roast fragments rewarmed.
Dreamt I witnessed Julie Andrews prove again
      (on Broadway or in
      samizdat screen-test
      outtakes) her mettle—
      a knowledge staggered
(it arrived in timed phases): my responsibility for proving
      what I'd witnessed
      lay at a 45-degree
      angle to her competence's
      Agnes Martin arroyo horizontality.

A line breached, a Cherbourg pinnacle, oneiric yet actual:
      woke to discover
      Michel Legrand had died.
Dream punctuation is too complex a topic to broach today.

That lonely aggrieved persecuted feeling when you post a photo
    you consider aesthetic/
    ethereal and it is deemed
    to violate community
    standards—verdict im-
    possible to appeal or reverse.
Man, clutching flattened cardboard box, shouts
    "Laissez-passer," voice
    hoarse, ravaged: then
    "Take it easy, guys":
    bilingual tragi-
    commotion, like dream

last night of early Callas Santuzza, voice cutting
    into stage flats, peristyle's
    parallax "Voi lo sapete"
a reinterpreted virginity enclosed by rhombus stain.
Dreamt mother-in-law criticized my dishwashing
    technique: I in-
    sufficiently valued
    her faux netsuke
    tea set. My father,

telephoning her beach cottage, used my childhood
    bedroom's princess phone:
    Channel 36 "The Perfect
    36" Bardot-fest poor
    reception UHF Sacramento
porn-hub of Reagan governor manse, my juvie

nudie-addiction a rebuke
Situationist-esque to fossil fuel's
stranglehold on *Volks*-libido. Time to read Wilhelm Reich?
Time to multiply passerby
orgasms? Stroke-utopia
Timothy Leary animism,
visionary jolt via taint?

# #26 [Read Martin Herbert]

Read Martin Herbert's *Tell Them I Said No*: essays
        on artists (including
        Christopher D'Arcangelo)
        who refused the art world.
Read Helen Epstein's *Children of the Holocaust.*
Straight guy in row D at Elaine May play itched his ass
        through black jeans
        while wife rolled
        her eyes in disdain.
Guest list for a party Gregory Battcock threw on 3/3/76
        included Jill Johnston,
        Lucy Lippard, Robert
        Rosenblum, Andy Warhol,
        Leo Steinberg, Charlotte
        Moorman, Linda Nochlin.

Failed to describe the devotional fizz of this list's
        locked time-
        capsule condensation.
Father accused a Veronica Lake lookalike of flirting
        with randy sailors
        at a baccalà dispensary.
"I'm shy on camera," says the garçon
        researching Gypsy Rose Lee.

Moiroloi is a mode, alas, beyond my lamentably
    parochial ken.

"My empathic capacities are stunted, unmag-
        nanimous, unattractively
    mercurial," he reflected
    after the begrudged funeral.
What's the difference between the filmed, the drawn,
    and the written line?
Arachnid-arrested by nude model jerking off with no
    visible or tactile
    intervention on my part.

Orange then blue streetlight reflection on rainy
        pavement proposes
    each soul makes
    identical music despite
    thwart-integument
    imposing belligerent isolation.
Bulge-eyed Balanchine-worthy writer's wrist–
    waist ratio brings out
    the slayed grandee in me.
If bereft, befriend a new grape:
    brilliantine, grenadine,
    incarnadine, acetylene.

# #27 [Dreamt I peed]

Dreamt I peed into a suitcase, for convenience,
    in my school office, then
    puzzled over how to
    dispose of the wet container.
Also dreamt I peed into my toiletry kit, containing nail clippers,
    sleeping pills, condoms,
    batteries, tiny paper fish
    that grew when immersed
    in water but perished
    when desecrated by unkind urine.
*Potemkin* became the unlit story I leaned on, water-glass facets
    carouseling an invitation
    to enjoy (despite anti-
    Semitism) J.P. Morgan–
    era champagne-swill
    speakeasy horse-latitude.
The app made me choose two desires: I picked bears
    and underwear, omitted
    otters, suits,
    and pups: I'll Jacob's-
    ladder later toward
    daimon-spangled specialties.

Nitwit blocked me: *being-blocked,*
  Dasein extinction foretaste.
Andrews's *Torn Curtain* outfits by Edith Head undo
  Communist bloc
  ennui: Paul Newman's
  sluggish jaw, Julie-averse.
EJ uses my favorite blue, which sits on silver
  with regal out-
  goingness, unashamed
  of a natal tendency
  to dominate kin.
Mash-note the dancer-pianist with Mickey Rooney
  curl-mop: "Your tongue's
  divided by a fey
  yet butch rivulet."


Rooney mixed with Daniel Barenboim: we (my people?) gather
  pathos like chiton
  folds, undulant,
  waiting for the burning
  bush to recognize me.
*Me* gussies up *us*: yen to be solo ^ cuirasses [v.] (queer
  asses) the col-
  lective homunitarian
  (homo-commune) impulse
  squelched like Divine's farts
  in Fresnes semen-crib.
Dreamt I played *Il Trovatore* record so loudly it
  dominated my nine-

story dormitory's
hollow stairwells—

sonic leakage shameful: why no sound
in halls, elevator?
Whose Manrico? Björling's?
Dreamt I trained to New Haven for medievalist's 95th birthday
party: prayed
I'd blend in, adjunct
pudding, Big Sur road-
curves stoking paranoia.
I became sister or girlfriend by skating to winter Province-
town, scallop-shore
curving its brined peril-
embrace. Parkinson's
neighbor, bottom, advertises
as "always available,"
weighs 100 lbs. Typo?

# #28 [The color yellow's]

The color yellow's importunate tendency to pose
    stamen-rhetorical
    questions: my eye
    omits the verboten "o."
Dreamt crafty Mildred Dunnock–esque French citoyenne stole
    Sontag manuscript
    (Genet essay draft)
    from my music stand when
    I shut my eyes to take
    a picture of Sontag-scrawl:
fingerpainted André Masson ligatures. Citoyenne hid manuscript
    in her aqua housedress, then
    threatened to run me over
    with her Baby Jane Peugeot.
At Singing Sands Beach I dared her rage-car to slay me:
    I reached into her housedress
    to retrieve the *Notre-Dame-*
    *des-Fleurs* Sontag-script
    revealing rare expression-
    ist prelude to a style later
    hardening into *Volcano.*

Dreamt artist-baby with speech impediment employed periodic
    sentences when interpreting
    mother-murals refusing
    to encircle and contain.
I hugged the artist-body into feral submission. Malted milk
    crumbs coated baby skin
    like Yayoi Kusama dots.
Dreamt Joan Didion draped YSL gold-purple jacket
    over a couch's
    arm near my exhi-
    bitionism: no lunch for me,
    and a dead mouse in the pantry.
Snubbed lookalike at café: Botox-smoothed brother-leer
    in Rambler wayback beheld
    doppelgänger's career-gangrene—
    my debut, too, a debacle.

What if my butt produced peanut butter—edible
    economic miracle,
    nutritional nirvana,
    supernal resource—
freak phenomenon paparazzi'd in *Scientific American*,
    *The Wall Street Journal*?
His cousin instantly exited life by falling
    off a ladder:
    heart attack pre-
    ceded and in-
    stigated plunge.

Moved by Moffo/Corelli *Carmen* and vague scent of marijuana
        by sere sidewalk's
        soiled snowbank.
Never gave proper credit to her "Seguidilla," only now
        reckoning its late majesty.
Seek nontoxic paint thinner, if nontoxicity exists: suspicious
        tingle on tongue
        augurs termination?

# #29 [Dreamt a *Sonnambula*]


Dreamt a *Sonnambula* aria ("Ah! non credea") audible
      in grocery store while
      I scrutinized olive
      oil bottles exploding:
we threw boxes on top of the volatile oil, to mitigate or
      disguise emergency.
Boyfriend sunbathed nude on winter driveway's rough
      rocks, behind station
      wagon. I refused
      to sing a minor
      role in *Tristan*: bird's nest
Gretel-like poised on desiccated tree-branch crook beckoned
      as emblem of promises
      I'd callously broken, kitchen
      door open to eschatological
      whirlwind, kids licking
      the unhygienic floor.


Barcelona chair, born in Brno's Villa Tugendhat,
      abstractly de-
      lineates diaspora.
Green fake-turf wedge, gimlet-glass-sized, winked
      at me from demolished
      sidewalk undergoing repair

without love by capitalists,
    their crudeness mine.
"Masc 4 masc" unnerves femme's I-iceberg—
    calving ego-
    splinters. Take
an ordinary word—*chartreuse*—and wrap it in aura
    by signaling secret
    exquisiteness with extra
    lip-and-teeth emphases.


Write a story about a woman walking through a field
    after the world ends.
Wedge myself into 1930s polyamorous entanglements
    (chez George Platt Lynes).
    Mimic Marsyas: embody
    a stripped, blown reed.
Glinka's *Life for the Tsar* (Gedda, Stich-Randall, Christoff)—
    belatedly discovering
    monaural vocalism *Homo*
    *sapiens* splendor-summit
    recorded 1957, year


before my birth. Dreamt a urine rectangle
    framed or dominated
    my regnant pubis, yours.
Richard Tucker *La Juive* martyr-aria oversees relinquishment
    of optical shibboleths
    preceding Cubism, easel's
    lip charismatically flotsam-flecked.

Heidi complimenting my butt (echo-memory) rhymes
        with electric outlet's lure:
        plugs and sockets, utopia
        limned the day Peter Tork died.

# #30 [The lamp competes]

The lamp competes with the moon. The moon bears
    responsibility for what
    the lamp neglects.
Noticed today, on a depleted building's face, two
    unaffiliated fragments
    of defunct signage:
    "JUDY," "Rainbow."
Misheard "tarte aux pommes" as "tarte homophobe."
    Dreamt Callas taught
    me how to breathe.
Serrated edge of bistre-colored candle provides
    Delphic immersion, moon-
    flame for footsie in Cambridge cave.


She celebrates the organ he desecrates—inward,
    pink, derided
    artistic signature:
    lurid *joie*-V.
Attention-fraying click-click-click of cameras
    near Van Gogh
    *Roses et anémones.*
Diction as drag, diction as ecstasy-catalyst, diction
    as hairpin, dic-
    tion as transitional object.

Misread "financial advisor" as "funeral advisor,"
    "Renaissance Hotel"
    as "Resistance Hotel."


Dreamt of NYC bombed, burning; scrutinized my
    belongings, said goodbye
    in panicked clear-sighted flashes.
Dreamt I found a magic ATM that disgorged $1,000 bills
    not rightfully mine.
Orphaned Floridian heiress bystander—her first-position
    ballet feet admonitory—
    telephoned the fuzz.


Dreamt I watched John Ashbery do a three-point turn,
    his Mini Cooper in
    a tight parking lot
    overlooking a gorge.
*Image* contains *I am* and *magi* and *age* and *me*.
    Imagine 1970
    margarine discovered today
    in a natural history museum.
White bath-towel, hanging askew, your pill-like pro-
    tuberances sever my
    capacity to be a guest lovingly
    tucked under anaesthesia's counterpane.

# #31 [Ode to Bromance]


Ode to Bromance. Ode to Trigger Warnings.
    Ode to Crocodile
    Tears. Ode to Canasta.
Willa Cather, won't a Cather. Sis is acidic,
    bro is Hasidic.
Bushwick Avenue, nighttime, two men stroking beards
    outside apartment
    building, seen
    from arrested car's window.
Dreamt little brother unplugged mother's
    Marvel stove and
    hurled it out the kitchen
    window: landing,

the stove exploded into flames. Mother cried
    when she witnessed
    the atrocity, a crime
I'd authorized by not preventing: why hadn't I tried
    to dissuade him from
    destroying maternal property?
Misread "professor of sociology" as "professor
    of apology."
Misread "concentrated" as "castrated."
    Ungeld homophonic glosses,
    sonic heterotopias for tots.

I sniffed Patrick Heron's 1966 painting (*Three Cadmiums*),
    toxic reds and oranges
    no longer odorous.
Unforgotten experience of being excoriated
    by a stranger, cloaking
    vindictiveness in ethics.
Saw a man bloodied at intersection, then a turtle
    lifted by stopped driver
    and repatriated to a pond.

I apply Unsettled's pineapple/labdanum notes
    to pulse points and become
    temporary, coincidental—
    a gravid ship
    espied by mariner-god's
    Etch-A-Sketch divination.
Dream, shame-daggered yet coldly procedural,
    about bathroom
    etiquette, hand-dryer error,
    toilet-stall overcrowding.
Cavort, O babies of the canyon: a spring-song imperative, ex-
    clamation, chord torn from
    larynx-lyre's lingual clay.

# #32 [Misread "master craftsman"]

Misread "master craftsman" as "nastier craftsman."
"To heck with rigor!" I shouted in a microphone—retort
    broadcast across
    the college green.
Large-featured prof, the hurried type
    that harrows me,
    mastered the toy
    store's revolving door.
Baptize my green sponge Cain. Cain
    wipes regular household
    surfaces. The blue
    sponge, Abel, reserved

for washing dishes, holds sway.
    (Jackie and Lee?) Dis-
    respectful analogies
    anoint domestic day.
Dreamt I drafted a tiny, three-chaptered Jewish book
    about *La Cérémonie*
    starring Isabelle Huppert.
Two spermatozoa commas on the ascending elevator's
    copper annunciation screen.
Tempestuous behavior of daffodils, arranged
    within a fenced rectangle.

Bird-cries befriend me on West 23rd Street without
    knowing who I am,
without caring whether I occupy a single body
    or several. Bird-
    carillons emerge
from multiple bird-bodies, none I've separately
    acknowledged. Reprieve
    from saying hello to each
    individual creature gives
    spring its identity-annulling oomph.

Dreamt a one-legged psychoanalyst took assiduous
    opinionated notes while
    I recounted my
    troubled history.
He divided my psyche into threes. Young woman reads
    Fitzgerald's *The Beautiful*
    *and Damned* as she
    waits in a flower district
traffic island for the illuminated "walk" sign to push
    her back into ordinary uncertain
    life, beautiful or damned.

# #33 [Oranges and onions]

Oranges and onions are hard to tell apart when wrapped in-
    cognito in orange
    plastic mesh sacks.
"Cinematogenic legs" I whispered after witnessing
    a blossoming pink
    magnolia tree in
    Washington Square Park.
Dogwood? Teach me botany, jogger
    who looked askance at
    my vernal expostulation.
In rain under checkered umbrella I write
    fragments while beholding
    pansies. If you are
    indeed pansies, please

speak up. Father and daughter on subway might be husband
    and wife—young woman
    snuggling her dad-
husband, torsos undulating on a stalled train.
    He wore a wedding ring.
    She didn't. Let's assume
    she wasn't his daughter,
despite their body language spreading incest-
    speculation clouds across

brows of commuting
onlookers, perplexed
or blessed by proximity

to the undefined. Lifelong wiggler, I strive
to morph into a maestro
of mesh jocks, thongs—
costumes for modeling
sessions, auto-portraits
sent to the No One.
Inbox of the No One, crowded with mesh-
exhibitionism missives
of jonquil longing, whatever
a jonquil looks like—

jonquil of ill repute, jonquil imagined while my back
is turned to the setting
sun, a view mas-
ochistically forfeited,
although to forfeit a pleasure is to claim, by reverse
proxy, the unseen.
From a paper bag, cut out a shape.
Paint on it with gouache.
Pin it to the wall. Give
the transformed scrap a title.
Cross out the title.
Replace it with a phrase
stolen from *Stolen Kisses.*

# #34 [Two quartered radishes]


Two quartered radishes, consumed
    while dressing
    for death: diminutive
    delicacies, deviations.
Caressed two words: *felucca* and *bromeliad.*
Confused between *intended* and *indented*:
    intended bride?
    indented bride?
Two weeks ago I trod a Notre Dame now burning.


Eviscerating windstorm. Hugged two more words:
    *janissaries* and *solan.*
So long, Janus-faced blueboy. Nice knowing your spirit
    lamp had no hold
    on my esophagus.
Topless man jogging past Gothic rowhouses dropped
    an "I want to erase
    you with my handsome
    aplomb" bomb.
Crackers at the ready and an uncooperative banana,
    its peel sluggish.

I ride the Internet sidesaddle; I stop to feed
　　the craving-matrix its oats.
Before groin-mirage of metempsychosis arose,
　　I entered the Book-
　　mobile's pharma-
　　ceutical cavern.
Father confesses: "You have a good life—you didn't
　　make the mistake
　　of having children."


Imagine melon in the mouth of Omar Sharif Jr.,
　　concocted crush. Lucky
or unlucky penny, poised on crack between urine-
　　scented subway
　　cement quadrants.
Assaulted by paper flyer (health store brochure) riding the air
　　behind my neck as I
　　descend to subway
　　and imagine tactile pleasure
　　of fingers landing
　　on minor and major
　　seconds in Persichetti
　　sonatina tonight I'll
　　imitate to excavate
　　what primordial clash?

# #35 [Space between shelved]

Space between shelved volumes (dream of laureate's library)
    permitted finger entrance—
    wrong-minded purchase
    of organic vegetables for
    shared untimely supper.
"What about Catherine Deneuve? She's more reachable, more
    in our circle of acquaintance.
    Ask her to star
    in our monodrama."
"Come here, I have dolls for you to play with," commanded
    nearby father's high-
    pitched voice.
Two bearded, apparently straight dudes talking about vitamin D
    and *Homo erectus*
    on the M train.


If perceptions misbeget I should squelch
    inklings before they
    ascend into speech.
Pink tree dithers outside the shopping mall. Which
    deserves pity—
    magnolia or mall?
Dubious catharsis: after spraying Citra Solv cleaner on a rag,
    nitrile-gloved hands
    investigate and wipe

months of dust from
radiator's honey-
combed crevices.
Wasted time watching YouTube videos about lobotomy
and past-life regression.

Over Lacryma Christi del Vesuvio, we plan
playlet starring Omar
Sharif Jr. and Anouk Aimée.
Write down an advice aphorism you accepted from Nietzsche
whether or not he
intended to give it.
Odors of daffodils and walnut cake,
mingled, approximate
cooked bacon,

heretical aphrodisiac. Men who spit on the sidewalk,
even if they wear pink
shirts, slaughter precarious
civic homeostasis.
Every new customer who slinks into this sanctuary
becomes a curiosity
or keepsake, a Chance
Wayne procured by last-
legs Alexandra Del Lago.
Dreamt a wounded poet told a wounded poet that in my writing
I always "queen it up."

# #36 [Methought her quibble]

Methought her quibble had a cuckold hymn.
If quibble has a name, the alias is tree
    or parachute.
Test the tree's personality by embracing its lichen
    and asking if the bark,
    motionlessly peripatetic,
    embodies percipience.
Tried to buy scar-concealing makeup at Sephora.
    Staff couldn't find
    a salve to sell me.


Young man I passed on the sidewalk, did you say
    to your companion
    "foray" or "Fauré"?
Odds are, "foray"; but when I heard—falsely—
    "Fauré," psyche quickened,
    and soma tagged along,
    fluttering in triplets.
What hallows a sidewalk? Discards.
    Bra, blender,
    vase, teddy bear,
    ashtray, Monopoly.

Rode an orange folding bike past
     the factory where they raise
     mice for medical experiments.


Mooned a Victorian mansion. These flowers I want
     you to see are
     gayfeathers.
To turn a person into a flower is to *hyacinthize*, a nonce verb.
Walking to the rosebush, I cut short
     a bespoke bunny's
     clover-nibbling. Reverse
     my steps, restore
     rabbit-hegemony.
     Undo accidental
     near-martyrdoms,
     oppose blood sacrifice.


Up my nose went the virus-testing spear, divination tendril,
     a tickle like bel canto's
     G-spot, or *Ballo in Maschera's*
     Ulrica—transubstantiating mezzo
     Marian Anderson finally sang.
I couldn't foreknow this feather would take three years to finish.
     Summarize the missing
     follicles, foehn-blown boy
     not yet a boy again. Boy identity
oscillates, subdivides, thrashes itself, breeds backward, unbarbs
     the calamus, unthreads
     the barbule. Thirteen

years old you are biking
calamitously toward rose-
garden memory-fulcrum, mother-
shrink outdoor staircase a Jacob's-
ladder tail tongue-hanging out my mouth,
open for wafers, recantation, apricots.

## Acknowledgments

I wish to thank the editors of the following publications (print and online), in which poems from this book, sometimes in different versions, first appeared:

*The Best American Poetry 2023* (edited by Elaine Equi): "#32 [Misread 'master craftsman']"

*The Experiment Will Not Be Bound*, ed. Peter Campion (Unbound Edition Press): "#5 [Frizz-hair poodle lapdance]"

*FENCE*: "#2 [Eye doctor wanted]," "#4 [Flatiron realness minus]"

*Harvard Review*: "#32 [Misread 'master craftsman']"

*The Iowa Review*: "#18 ['Roar of God']," "#24 [Beard smooth skin]"

*KGB Bar Lit*: "#8 [O razor in]," "#25 [Seen, discarded in]," "#28 [The color yellow's]"

*Mantis*: "#1 [How men eat]"

*Modern Queer Poets*, ed. Richard Porter (Pilot Press): "#13 [Bedside lamp reflection]"

*New American Writing*: "#3 [59th anniversary today]," "#26 [Read Martin Herbert]," "#27 [Dreamt I peed]"

*The Poetry Project*: "#17 [Older I get]"

*Revel*: "#6 [The artist sang]," "#20 [My inexplicable bruise]," "#29 [Dreamt a *Sonnambula*]," "#36 [Methought her quibble]"

*Venti*: "#9 [Regret's a clod]," "#10 [Upload to private]," "#19 [Blue tape seam]"

*Volt*: "#30 [The lamp competes]"

Thank you to Hedi El Kholti, for giving Semiotext(e)'s blessing to scapegoat and stubble, sonnet and story. Thank you to PJ Mark, for guiding my voyage between genres. Thank you to Zachary Pace, for scrutinizing the vessel and fixing its leaks.